D0853317

THE
NINE DAYS WONDER
(THE OPERATION DYNAMO)

ALSO BY JOHN MASEFIELD

PLAYS:

THE FAITHFUL: *A Tragedy in Three Acts*
GOOD FRIDAY: *A Play in Verse*
ESTHER *(Adapted and partially translated from the French of Jean Racine)*
BERENICE *(Adapted from the French of Jean Racine)*
MELLONEY HOLTSPUR; or, The Pangs of Love: *A Play in Four Acts*
A KING'S DAUGHTER: *A Tragedy in Verse in Four Acts*
THE TRIAL OF JESUS
THE TRAGEDY OF NAN
TRISTAN AND ISOLT: *A Play in Verse*
THE COMING OF CHRIST
EASTER: *A Play for Singers*
END AND BEGINNING

POETRY:

DAUBER
THE DAFFODIL FIELDS
PHILIP THE KING AND OTHER POEMS
LOLLINGDON DOWNS AND OTHER POEMS, WITH SONNETS
A POEM AND TWO PLAYS *(Rosas, a poem; The Locked Chest, The Sweeps of Ninety-Eight)*
REYNARD THE FOX
ENSLAVED AND OTHER POEMS
RIGHT ROYAL
SELECTED POEMS
KING COLE AND OTHER POEMS
COLLECTED POEMS
MIDSUMMER NIGHT AND OTHER TALES IN VERSE
MINNIE MAYLOW'S STORY AND OTHER TALES AND SCENES
A TALE OF TROY
A LETTER FROM PONTUS AND OTHER VERSE
SOME VERSES TO SOME GERMANS

FICTION:

SARD HARKER
ODTAA
THE MIDNIGHT FOLK
THE HAWBUCKS
THE BIRD OF DAWNING
THE TAKING OF THE GRY
THE BOX OF DELIGHTS
VICTORIOUS TROY
EGGS AND BAKER
THE SQUARE PEG
DEAD NED
LIVE AND KICKING NED
BASILISSA

GENERAL:

GALLIPOLI
THE OLD FRONT LINE
ST. GEORGE AND THE DRAGON
THE BATTLE OF THE SOMME
RECENT PROSE
WITH THE LIVING VOICE
THE WANDERER OF LIVERPOOL
POETRY: *A Lecture*
THE CONWAY

THE
NINE DAYS WONDER

(THE OPERATION DYNAMO)

BY

JOHN MASEFIELD

NEW YORK

THE MACMILLAN COMPANY

1941

FIRST PRINTING.

PRINTED IN THE UNITED STATES OF AMERICA
AMERICAN BOOK—STRATFORD PRESS, INC., NEW YORK

This tale is dedicated
to
Vice-Admiral Sir BERTRAM RAMSAY, K.C.B., M.V.O.
to
The Officers, Warrant-Officers and Ratings,
and to all others who bore a hand
in the Operation Dynamo.

ILLUSTRATIONS
(to be found at end of book)

PREFACE

THIS pamphlet gives a summary of the lifting of the First French Army and the B.E.F. from the beaches of Dunquerque.

Probably, every man of those armies knew that the success of the enemy was due to great numbers of aeroplanes, tanks and guns.

Our own soldiers knew, too, that the enemy had profited by extraordinary miscalculations for which no British soldier was in any way responsible. As a part of an Allied Army Group, the B.E.F. had been ordered forward to attack. They had hardly reached the attacking positions before the Army on their left flank was gravely compromised, and the Army on their right flank threatened. Three days later, the Army on their left flank was falling back and the Army on their right flank was broken through. At once, the B.E.F. found itself with its right flank turned, its left flank in danger, and its communications imperilled. It was in the most dangerous position that the war offered. Those who had imperilled it had foreseen nothing of the kind and were unable to improvise measures to kill the danger. There was nothing for it but to fall back, and falling back was made almost impos-

sible from the first by the multitudes of refugees on
the roads. Our men could only crawl back, while the
enemy raced to cut them from the sea.

It had been a part of the enemy's plan to block the
roads with escaping citizens; this plan was helped by
a want of decision among the Belgian authorities, who
strove, indeed, but did or could not stop this use of
the roads by the multitudes seeking safety. Among
those multitudes, some millions in number, were always countless skilled enemy spies, carrying small
wireless transmitters by which they reported the presence of troops.

On the roads so blocked, our Army moved in one
of the most difficult and dangerous operations in war,
a long withdrawal with both flanks in danger and
communications hampered, if not cut.

This withdrawal took them through a kind of cor-
ridor, the south wall of which was always being attacked and endangered by enemy tanks, while the
north wall was always threatened by the armies pressing our Belgian allies to breaking-point.

The story of the withdrawal will be told in detail
in time to come, when the papers of four Nations are
sorted and printed, perplexities have been resolved,
and many, now prisoners of war, have returned to tell
their tales. It must suffice now, to say, that in the
chaos caused by the enemy's great success against the
French Ninth Army, our soldiers instantly, with
fore-thought and resource, improvised defences for
the threatened flanks, so that the withdrawal might

be made without disaster. This fore-thought and resource have not yet been recognised by the world nor
praised as they deserve.

The enemy attacked Belgium and Holland on the
10th May; by the 15th, he had broken the French
line and was advancing towards the sea. Our army
fell back to the line of the Escaut.

On Sunday, May the 19th, a meeting was held in
London to "consider the maintenance of the B.E.F.
through Dunquerque, Calais and Boulogne, and sec-
ondly, the possible evacuation, which was considered
to be unlikely, through those three ports."

On Tuesday, May the 21st, another meeting was
held, "to consider the emergency evacuation of very
large forces, the necessity for air-protection, and the
need of a large number of small boats to carry troops
to the off-shore ships."

By the 23rd of May, the enemy had taken Abbeville, cut the line of the Somme, invested Boulogne
and Calais, and was so heavily bombing Dunquerque
that the port could not easily be used. All the ports
supplying our Army were therefore useless to us; our
Army was short of supplies and could no longer be
sure of obtaining any. Our men drew back towards
the coast, closely pressed by the enemy, heavily
bombed by his powerful air-force, threatened at all
points by skilfully used tanks, and hampered everywhere by the jams of traffic and of refugees on the
roads.

Boulogne fell in the morning of the 24th May. The

enemy, for the moment, contained Calais, and prepared to cut our retreating Army from Dunquerque by sending tanks against the Aire Canal, which
made the main defence of its endangered right flank.

The defence of this flank against continual attack
by an enemy outnumbering them in tanks and
bomber-aircraft brought much glory to the commands
engaged.

On the 25th of May, the enemy cut or bombed out
of action the waterworks which supplied Dunquerque.
There were still a good many wells in the district,
but by this time many canal sluices thereabouts had
been opened to make inundations on the west and
south of the city. These floods in a day or two made
the ground sufficiently soft to check tanks. Unfortunately, by that time the water began to seep into all
the wells and make them brackish. This was soon to
add to the troubles of our soldiers; who were short
of water in the last hot days of the campaign.

In the evening of this day the German High Command announced to the foreign newspaper corre-
spondents with its armies that "the ring around the
British, French and Belgian Armies has been defi-
nitely closed."

On Sunday, the 26th of May, enemy bombs set fire
to the oil-tanks in Dunquerque; they burned till the
end of the campaign. At 6.57 in this evening, the
preparations made for lifting troops from Dunquerque were put into practice; some of the base-units
were removed to England, and the beach-parties

arranged for more to follow soon. This operation was given the name of Dynamo.

Calais fell at almost the same time.

On the 27th, our Belgian Allies, after losing very heavily against a better-equipped Army, surrendered. This surrender opened our left flank to the enemy; its effect upon the French people was very grave.

Our Army was now retreating into the bridgehead or perimeter of Dunquerque, where Nature and art together had made a very strong position between the sea and a system of canals.

The position is closed on the north-east by the canals and forts between Nieuport and Furnes. It is closed on the south-east by the canals and forts between Dunquerque and Bergues.

A big canal, linking Bergues with Furnes, makes a moat across its landward side. All the space enclosed thus between canals and the sea is much cut about with rhines and waterways.

It has one very great advantage. It is cut into two halves by the fortified French frontier in such a way that we could yield the eastern half to the enemy and yet hold a strong fortress in the western half. This fact was of much importance to us towards the end of the adventure.

The outer line of this bridgehead was now strengthened with what guns could be found. It was arranged that the 1st Corps of the B.E.F. should march into the west, the 2nd Corps of the B.E.F. into the east side of the enclosed space.

Dunquerque, being an important French city, was held to the end by what remained of the Seventh French Army. It was arranged that the First French Army should march into a part of the western side of the space, to that great suburb of Dunquerque known as Malo-les-Bains.

While these defences were being garrisoned the less-needed units of the B.E.F. were taking ship for England.

Meanwhile, the enemy made great efforts to burst in the defences of our flanks, to break through our front, and to bomb us to ruin from overhead.

During the days of the lifting, the defences of the flanks and front, so that the armies might embark, became sublime feats of war.

Not less sublime, and as yet equally unpraised were the efforts of the Royal Air Force to check the enemy bombing.

At an early stage in the campaign, the enemy had made it impossible for our Air Force to use any aerodrome north of the latitude of Abbeville. This did not matter much to our bomber command, but it was very serious to the fighter aircraft with restricted ranges of action. These had to be based upon England, and could not stay long over France in any sortie.

Some have written, that while they were near Dunquerque, they seldom saw our fighting aircraft, though they daily saw many of the enemy. It is true, that our airmen were always outnumbered by the enemy, but

their unceasing, heroic and successful efforts to check
the enemy bombing were among the main marvels of
the time.

A little thought will show the reader that any effective checking of bombing must take place some miles
from the target aimed at by the bomber, that is, long
before he can be in a position to drop his bombs with
effect.

The main defences of the Dunquerque beaches
against bombers were anti-aircraft guns on or near the
beaches. Our defending fighter and bomber squadrons and patrols always sought to intercept and scatter
the enemy bombers long before they could arrive over
the beaches. They were most successfully active in this
when they were least likely to be seen by men on the
beach.

During the nine days, they certainly destroyed or
shot down 377 enemy machines with a loss to themselves of 87 machines.

With this preliminary note the tale of the lifting
may begin. Our Army and the First French Army
were withdrawing within the perimeter; our Navy
was beginning to carry them to safety.

They marched over the Field of Waterloo,
By Goumont and La Haie, and then fell back,
Forever facing front to the attack
Across the English bones.

Westward, by Fontenoy, their ranks withdrew;
The German many bomb-bursts beat the drum,
And many a trooper marched to kingdom come
Upon the Flanders stones.

Westward they went, past Wipers, past the old
Fields bought and paid for by their brothers' blood.
Their feet were in the snapping of the flood
That sped to gulf them down.

They were as bridegrooms plighted to the mould
Those marching men with neither hope nor star,
The foeman in the gateways as a bar,
The sea beyond to drown.

And at the very sea, a cloud of night,
A hail of death and allies in collapse,
A foe in the perfection of his traps,
A certainty of doom.

When, lo, out of the darkness, there was light,
There in the sea were England and her ships,
They sailed with the free salt upon their lips
To sunlight from the tomb.

DUNQUERQUE

DUNQUERQUE is an ancient sea-port, with a good depth of water, several docks, some building-slips, and the sea-mouths of three big canals. The city lies within a ring of old ramparts, all amply moated. Outside it, the coast stretches away to the east-north-east towards the Belgian frontier and Nieuport, the one eight, the other sixteen, miles away.

This stretch of coast does not vary much in all those miles. Near the sea is an expanse of broad, shelving sand, in peace-time summers always thronged by multitudes of bathers. To shoreward there are digues, or sea-walls, of brick, and beyond them the sand-dune country, with rough sea-grass, a few poplars, a few windmills, and many drainage-channels. The sand-dunes change their shapes a good deal in heavy weather. To landward from the dunes there is a stretch about a mile broad where scrub and brush grow.

Within the last half century the stretch of beach has been much improved for the benefit of summer visitors. There are hotels, places of amusement, and a good coast road. Outside the walls of Dunquerque, to the east, is the seaside suburb of Malo-les-Bains, with a big Kursaal and Casino. Farther along the beach is a lesser pleasure place, Bray Dunes, also with a large Casino; and still farther to the east-north-east is the village of La Panne. This was at one time much visited by painters. In the Great War it became famous as the headquarters of King Albert of Belgium. In its churchyard there lies the body of a Belgian lady who was one of the victims of the *Lusitania*.

Though the coast may allure in the summer, it can be exceedingly dangerous both to seaman and landsman. In stormy winter weather one walking on the beach will be astounded by the violence of the surf and the distance to which its breakers stretch. As in parts of Holland, he will feel at such times, that the sea is really above the land and may at any time engulf it.

The coast shelves gradually into the sea all along the beach. About three-quarters of a mile from low-water-mark there is the deep-water channel of the Rade de Dunquerque, with a steady depth of from forty to fifty feet, and a width of about half a mile. To seaward from this again are successions of sandbanks, some of them awash at low water, and all of them marine museums rich with the relics of ships.

"Oh, combien de marins, combien de capitaines." These shoals make a good protection to ships anchored in the Rade.

The tidal streams are often very strong here. Any northerly gale or fresh wind raises a dangerous sea upon the beaches and across the harbour entrance whenever it comes against a tide; an easterly gale will make an awkward sea at the harbour entrance. When a surf is running it breaks some distance from the shore, looks evil, and is much more evil than it looks.

Even in peace-time the deep-water approach to the port is not easy after dark. It is somewhat narrow for tides so strong. In war-time, when the navigation-beacons are extinguished, it may be very difficult. In the present war, before the lifting of the B.E.F. began, certain ships had already laid their bones near the entrance to the harbour.

Piety in old time raised lofty towers to the churches near the coast here, to be guides to mariners. These towers still stand. They are impressive from the low-ness of the land from which they spring, though per-haps modern man uses them more as artillery obser-vation posts than as sea-marks.

On the north side of the harbour of Dunquerque the ramparts are shut from the sea by a canal mouth fenced with a stone causeway about 900 yards long, known as the Promenade de la Digue. From the sea-ward end of this Promenade a strong wooden pier thrusts to the north-north-west into the sea; it is called the Jetée de l'Est: from its start from the Promenade it is about 1,400 yards long. From the beaches already described, from this long pier, and from the jetty to the west of the harbour the Allied Armies were lifted during the last week of the campaign.

Most of them marched along the East Pier, or Mole, a "five-foot-wide wooden pathway", which remained a way until the end, in spite of all that the enemy could do. Commander J. C. Clouston, R.N., who was its pier-master for a week (a record of great glory) was unhappily lost on June 1st. Some hundreds of men were killed and wounded on this pier; at least a quarter of a million reached safety by it.

Just one week after the first meeting held to consider the possibility of an evacuation from Dunquerque it became clear that the lifting must begin at once and continue with all possible speed.

Preparations of different kinds had been made during that week. A number of naval officers and seamen had been ordered for duty as beach-masters and beach parties; the Movement Control and Ministry of Shipping officials had also been busy. Troopships, hospital ships, supply ships and other craft had been detailed. All the enormous work of getting ready had been begun.

The Senior Naval Officer in charge of the Operation on shore at Dunquerque was Captain W. G. Tennant, C.B., M.V.O., R.N.

The docks at Dunquerque could now only be used by small vessels, as ships had been bombed and sunk within the Main Basin. In any case, the dock area was too hot from the burning warehouses and oil-fuel-tanks for men to use it much. Ships could still go alongside the wall in the Tidal Basin, but the approaches to it were made almost impassable by the intense heat and the continuous bombing. There remained only the East Pier, which had not been built for the berthing of ships, and might well give way under the strain of several thousand tons butting against it on a windy night. It had been built, in the main, as a groyne.

There were no piers along the nine or ten miles of beach, either to the east or west. Since embarkation from the pier alone would not suffice to lift the numbers in time, it was planned that the men should get into boats upon the beaches and be ferried to ships anchored in the channel off the shore. For many days a great deal of boat traffic had plied between ships and the beach. As the port proper could not be used, owing to the fires and bombing, our Army was largely supplied by such means; its bread, meat, drink and ammunition were landed there from boats, and still had to be landed.

Some foreign critics have written that it should have been easy for a maritime race, only forty miles from Dunquerque, to improvise a swift, effective service of ships and boats, and to lift the Army in a day.

War has a way of complicating even the simplest movement; and this was never a simple movement. Even in peace the business would not have been too easy. Tell even a skilled contractor that he is to send shipping forty-odd miles to ship over three hundred thousand men within a fortnight from one beach and one jetty, and bring them back the forty-odd miles; give him one week for preparation and another week for the deed, and how likely would he be to do it?

In peace the contractor would only have to tele-phone to hire shipping; he would be free to work without interruption, all would be easy, yet how many contractors in this world would be able to do it? Can you name one?

In war it is not easy to telephone to hire shipping. Every ship that can swim is in use in important na-tional service; every boat is precious, and every life-boat round the coast is on duty. Every small coast-wise vessel is on duty that cannot be interrupted without danger. To gather a great number of ships in a hurry, to man them, equip them with instru-ments, charts, food, water, fuel, weapons and ammu-nition, is most difficult.

The forty miles of the journey were already subject to violent and continual attack from the air through-out, to danger from magnetic, floating and moored mines, to attack from submarines and motor-torpedo-boats.

These were but some of the complications which war gave to the problem. The greatest complications were the war itself, with its ever-changing face and the fact that we were tied to Allies; each with urgent needs which were not necessarily ours. No man knew what the situation would be within the next few hours, and each of the three Allies wanted different things at once. The Belgians wanted us on their right flank; the French wanted us on their right flank; we wanted both of them to fall back quickly to end the very dangerous situation in which they stood; but both, being on their native soil, wished to stay where they were. At this end of the campaign it was almost impossible to get news from these two armies, or even to learn where their headquarters lay. News or suggestions sent from either might be fifteen hours on the road, and come so late that both would be useless.

When the Operation Dynamo began it was thought that only a few thousand could be saved. The next day the situation was so much worse that we had to be prepared for a desperate scramble to pick up survivors from a great disaster. After this, as all the rearguard actions so heroically fought had staved off the disaster, it was thought that the whole B.E.F. might be saved. But on the fifth day, when special effort was being made to lift the rearguard of the B.E.F., the whole arrangement was cancelled so that the French might be brought to England instead. The numbers given to the Officer-in-Command were "forty to fifty thousand". Later a hundred and fifty thousand or more were mentioned figures; in the end rather more than a hundred and twenty-three thousand Frenchmen were brought to England. This made the entire operation at least one-third bigger than anyone had thought possible, and this enormous increase in the work came suddenly upon those responsible after five frightful days, and at a time when death and destruction had thinned out the beach parties and smashed and sunk countless boats and many ships. The survivors were almost at the last gasp, the men were worn out, and nearly all the ships were in need of overhaul. It was upon these over-strained units that the extra work fell most heavily. It was this rising to the extra work right at the end which made the Operation Dynamo so magnificent a deed.

The pier at Dunquerque was under heavy attack continually; gaps were frequently bombed in it, and these had to be repaired with what could be found—ships' gangways, naval mess tables, etc. The beach had problems of its own. To begin with, the Army had not been trained for embarkation from an open beach, and some of it, when it reached the beach, was disorganised, by the mixing up of units. Many men came into the perimeter after marching all night on roads jammed and blocked by transport. In the darkness and confusion they had become lost; a few units had no officers, a few officers had no men. In any case, not many soldiers are used to boat-work, few have practised getting into boats from three or four feet of water when in uniform; nor is this feat easy, even in quiet water. It is a feat very difficult to do under heavy fire by men who have marched and fought with little sleep or food for seventeen days on end. The footing is firm sand, but whenever the tide ebbs and the wind sets on shore there is a swirl which makes boat-loading very hard.

Most of the embarkation had to be done by small ships, because only these could lie near the shore or enter the channel at low water. All ships coming near to the coast were bombed. A bomb bursting near a small ship nearly always disarranged or broke some of her gear. In some cases the engines were lifted from their beds; gauges and fans were smashed, compasses dismantled or deranged, and feed-pipes broken. The losses in men were very great; in ships, severe, and in boats enormous. Those ordering this adventure in Dover had daily to replace men and repair or replace ships; for probably no ship returned from the beach undamaged. The minds which improvised this service had to be prepared for great losses which were certain to grow as the embarkation proceeded. Nothing but enormous heroic industry and utter self-sacrifice kept the ships steadily plying to and fro. The operation called into use 125 maintenance craft, in addition to all the carriers, for the maintenance alone was a nightmare. All the ships had to be refuelled. They were of many different types gathered anyhow; they needed many different kinds of coal, or oil or spare fittings. They had to be provisioned and watered, not only for their crews, but for the multitudes they had to bring. They needed an incredible number of rafts, ladders, brows, life-buoys and grasslines. Often a ship's supplies of these things would be shot away in her first trip, and new ones had to be found on her return. Many thousands of the men brought were wounded. These had to have instant attention and special removal. Hundreds of the dead had to be landed for burial. New officers, crews, engine-room staffs and stokers had often to be found to take the places of the exhausted, the hurt and the dead. Many of the ships pressed into service had to be fitted with instruments; they had not even adjusted compasses. All had to be supplied somehow with duplicate drafts of the channels leading to Dunquerque harbour; and as these channels varied with the passing of time and the sinking of ships at new points, these drafts and track-charts had to be altered and marked.

It must be remembered that the ships and boats of all kinds only started to arrive after the order for evacuation had been given and the work had begun. The work, and the organisation of the work, had to proceed together. At one time there were as many as a hundred and fifty craft anchored outside Dover Harbour, while another fifty waited in the Downs for orders and supplies.

Knowing some of the difficulties, I should say that the Operation was the greatest thing this nation has ever done.

Sunday, the 26th of May.

When the first troopships sailed for Dunquerque in the afternoon, it had been arranged that two ships should call every four hours at the jetty, while drifters should stay off the beaches to receive men ferried out by motor-launches. The first ship of the Operation returned to Dover with troops at 10.30 that night; her load was of 1,312 base units and lines of communication men.

Dunquerque had been frequently and heavily bombed daily and nightly for some weeks; it was on fire in many places, and blazing to heaven from its oil-tanks. For the next week bombs must have fallen on or near it every five minutes. It was reckoned that in the Great War it received in all some 7,600 bombs; this record (though considerable) was easily passed now, for the enemy sent over immense flights, in the almost certainty of success.

Wherever his bombers flew they had a perfect target beneath them, columns crowded on roads, shipping crowded in a channel, masses of men upon a beach. During the week there were three hundred and fifty thousand men shut in within a narrow compass with all their possessions; any bomb dropping anywhere inside the perimeter was certain to be destructive. These bombers and their masters exulted at the sight. For the first time a great German encircling movement was to be helped to complete triumph by mastery in the air. Sedan had been a victory; this was to be an annihilation.

Monday, the 27th of May.

At an early hour the enemy began his effort to annihilate. Nelson said long ago: "Only numbers can annihilate": the enemy had the numbers. He had us penned in within a ditch and the sea; death was round three sides of us and above us: and no doubt death came down upon us. What our men faced in those days is hard to imagine.

The enemy had long boasted (and had paid others to boast) of the overwhelming might of his air force. He had the might: no doubt of that: he had the target of his dreams, and the prize of a century. No other place in the war offered such a prize. By putting all his bombers on to the beaches and the harbour entrance all day and all night long for one week of time he might do something which would fill all the headlines of the Press of the world.

The people of this island have never cared much for the headlines of the Press: in their dumb way they have cared a good deal for what will look well in a ballad. Now, when the enemy bombers came over in their numbers to annihilate, the little groups of our fighters took them on. Our fighters were few and could not stay over the beaches for more than fifteen to twenty minutes at a time: in countless cases they returned to England on their last gallon of petrol: but while they were over the beaches each little group would tackle fifty. The usual enemy formation was of ten to twenty bombers, with protecting fighters above them "arranged in steps", sometimes fifty strong. One British pilot, on this 27th, reports meeting a formation of between forty and fifty enemy fighters; he attacked them single-handed and made them split up. Another attacked six German bombers single-handed, and having fired off all his ammunition on them had to break off the battle; as he did so he ran into fifteen enemy fighters. He went into cloud to avoid these, having now no means of fighting; and came out of the cloud on to another twelve with the first fifteen still close behind him. He promptly made for more cloud, but, before he could reach it, was attacked by yet another twelve coming from the west. The skilful enemy often fled to draw our fighters into traps. "The enemy led us into very concentrated A.A. fire, which was very accurate up to a height of two miles and more. Tracer and flaming bullets which left a pink trail were observed to stream past very close. We carried out aerobatics to evade the A.A. fire, which was intense and had a very demoralising effect upon us." Still, at the end of the day one of these "very demoralised" men attacked forty enemy planes single-handed over the beach. Always in these days our fighters were so greatly outnumbered that they were hardly noticed by the men on the beaches whom they helped to save.

One of the drawbacks of fighting over the beaches was that if the aviator had to take to his parachute and drift slowly down, he became a target for many thousands of Belgian, British and French soldiers who imagined him to be a "parachutist". One man so floating down reckoned that twenty thousand rounds were fired at him as he came; all missing. Another says: "As I floated down I gave the Belgian soldiers and peasants five minutes' simple pleasure by acting as a target. Fortunately, their skill was not greater than their intelligence, and I was rescued by the

B.E.F. One enthusiast even took a last shot at me while I was talking to the officer".

This 27th was a bad day for the lifting of the troops. Calais had fallen the night before. The enemy lost no moment in seizing and equipping the good gun positions on the high ground at Les Hemmes and in manning the guns in the French fort of Grand Philippe. He opened fire with these upon the ships trying to enter Dunquerque by the usual passage from the west. His fire was so heavy and so accurate from these points that five transports had to turn back, a sixth was badly hit, and a seventh, while being shelled, was bombed from the air and sunk. This showed those in command that the short western route to the harbour could now only be used in darkness. There was nothing for it but to send the transports right round the French and English mine-fields so as to enter Dunquerque from the east by what is known as the Zuydecoote Pass. This route made the round voyage 172 miles instead of 80. Unfortunately the mine-sweepers had not finished the sweeping of this route; still, the need was so great that it had to be used. At the same time mine-sweepers were at once sent to sweep a shorter channel across the shoals and mine-fields between the beaches and England. This shorter route, when ready, made the round voyage 108 miles, but the sweeping and buoying took some time, and was not completed till the 28th. The enemy well knew what was being done and sent bombers on to both routes to sink the sweepers.

In other ways the day was disastrous. Two strings of valuable boats were lost. They were being towed to the beaches by tugs before dawn; in the darkness the tows were run down and the boats scattered. This was especially unfortunate, because there was a great shortage of boats suitable for beach work. There were thirty small ships off the beaches receiving men, but so few boats that they had to use their own. The cry of the day was for boats of the whaler type (sharp at both ends) and for skilled boatmen. The naval beach-parties were of the greatest possible help. Most of them passed most of this day up to their waists in water helping soldiers into boats. All the time the enemy bombers were bombing and machine-gunning the workers.

The results of the day were not encouraging. Five troopships took from the harbour 3,952 men between them. The drifters, using ship's boats, lifted some-thing like another 2,000 men from the beaches. A day's total of 6,000 men, when there were more than 300,000 to lift, was such a poor score that many peo-ple began to think that the operation would be a failure. The weather prospects were not too good. There was a heavy-weather system in the Atlantic: it seemed to be moving north: but if it moved even a little to the east, it might raise such a sea that the boats would be unable to ply upon the beaches.

Tuesday, the 28th of May.

We were lucky, because the storm passed to the north along the west coast of Ireland; only the extreme fringe of its secondary was felt in the Channel. However, even the fringe was bad enough. A surf got up on the beaches and swamped a good many boats, besides being most exhausting to the boats' crews. Other boats were lost by the lack of skilled boatmen. Soldiers coming off in boats often let them drift away as soon as they had reached a ship. The problem of embarkation was made more complex by the fact that on this day the beaches had to be used for the landing of water. By this time there was an acute shortage of drinking water in Dunquerque and on all the beaches; not less than 150,000 men were thirsty there. At least 50,000 more men, the entire Third Corps, were expected at the La Panne beach, and water had to be found. The ships contrived to land a good deal in tanks and petrol-tins.

All through the day our fighter squadrons continued their efforts to check the enemy bombing. There are several accounts of flights of three British pilots attacking formations of fifty enemy aircraft. One flight of three attacked a formation of seventy-two. One man mentions coming into forty-five bombers guarded by fighters engaged in dive-bombing the ships and craft just off the shore. Frequently our airmen met formations of thirty bombers attended by twenty fighters. In the afternoon, when the enemy made a very great and terrible bombing attack, one man counted ninety-five enemy aeroplanes over the beaches at once.

By this time there was so much smoke from the burnings over Dunquerque and the beaches that it was difficult for the enemy to see what was going on. Still, we lost on this day two trawlers by mines, two drifters and a troopship by bombs, and one minesweeper sunk in collision.

During the day some skoots approaching the harbour entrance were hailed by a skoot coming out. The hailer said that Dunquerque had now fallen into German hands and that the evacuation was over. This report was not due to enemy guile, but to a misunderstanding of what some soldier had said.

Wednesday, the 29th of May.

The troopships used the inner side of the East Pier throughout the day. A naval officer has described what he saw on these occasions. The first things seen by him, as his ship went along the eastern pass, were what seemed to be vast black shadows on the pale sands. In front of him, as he went in, was the blackness of smoke with tongues of flame shooting into it. On the sands were these blacknesses; he could not think what they were.

As it grew lighter he saw that the blacknesses were

enormous formations of men standing, waiting. He
saw them thus whenever he entered the pass, coming
or going. They did not seem to change; they did not
seem to sit, nor to lie down; they stood, with the
patience of their race, waiting their turn. He was
present throughout the evacuation. The thing which
impressed him most in all the week was this thing
which had so impressed him so deeply at the first, the
patient presence of these thousands, silently waiting,
among the racket of bombing, shelling and machine-
gunning, the roar of planes, guns, rifles and fires.

In the day-time there was both work and pleasure
on the beaches. Water, food and ammunition were
landed and carried up; the sick and wounded were
carried down; meals were cooked and eaten; the
troops under orders to embark formed and marched
to their embarkation points. One or two who were
there mention football on the beaches, "trick-riding
on military bicycles" and "pleasure-paddling". All
through the days of the evacuation the troops came
flooding into the perimeter, Belgians in some number, the First French Army, and more and more of
the B.E.F. All agreed that the bombing, though atro-
cious, continual and very trying, was not very deadly.
One man said: "If ever I have to be bombed again,
give me a sandy beach, for the bomb sinks in and
hurts very few when it bursts."

Three witnesses agree that the first days of the
evacuation were the worst, partly because the machine
had not begun to work smoothly, either from the lack

of equipment or from the failure of troops and boats
to arrive when each needed the other, and partly because the first men lifted were not always soldiers,
they were camp-keepers, store-keepers, drivers, and
lines of communication men. "The men became better and better as the evacuation continued. After the
first day the men were nearly all well behaved, patient and orderly. On the last two days they were
superb."

"It was wonderful to see them at the end, almost
dead-beat, but clean shaven and some of them sing-
ing."

"The French soldiers took longer to embark than
ours; they never liked to embark save as complete
units." "They were extraordinarily thoughtful; often
we could not get them to share our rations, as they
thought that we were short of food."

A naval officer, who was there, says that throughout
the evacuation an elderly British soldier stood at the
seaward end of the pier, quite unmoved by anything
that was happening. In peace-time such a figure would
have stood selling evening papers; this man seemed
to do nothing save collect rifles.

At the shoreward end of the East Pier was a deep
and very good cellar, where many men sheltered and
many wounded were treated. Throughout the evacuation an English woman lived in this cellar. It was said
that she was a London woman whose family lived in
Dunquerque. She was always cheery and helpful,
looking after the wounded, and making tea for the

weary. It is hoped by many that she reached England safely.

The weather during this 29th May was bad. One of the nuisances of the day was the density of the smoke about the harbour entrance. As the surf was running on most of the beach the harbour had to be used for the chief embarkations; so much black smoke from the burnings was driving down that the harbour entrance was often very difficult to find. Men in the harbour could not see what lay in the roads. One naval officer reported that there were no destroyers in the roads; as a matter of fact, there were then ten present. The men ordered for embarkation marched along the long wooden gangway of the East Pier to the ships. The smoke screened them from the sight of the enemy bombers, but many bombs were dropped at random on to them. The enemy was now shelling the harbour heavily, though not very accurately; he could not observe the bursting of his shells. Two of our destroyers were torpedoed in the early hours of the morning while bound for Dover laden with troops. The loss of lives was very heavy. Our ships opened fire on a vessel to the south-west; she blew up with a bright flash. She was thought to have been the enemy motor-torpedo-boat which sank our ships.

During the afternoon the embarkation was going fairly well, at the rate of about two thousand men an hour. The smoke was now a little clearer; a shift of wind was setting it inland. We had ten ships inside the pier, loading men, and four other ships waiting to come in. As this made a target which the enemy observers could not fail to see, a great force of bombers was sent against it. For two and a half hours, from about four o'clock, it rained bombs on the harbour entrance; and grievous harm was done.

Three of the ships at the pier got clear, much damaged; three were set on fire; one of these burning ships, the *Grenade,* seemed about to sink in the fairway; no doubt she would have sunk but for prompt action: a trawler towed her luckily clear in time. The *Verity,* coming out of the harbour entrance, struck on a sunken drifter and nearly added her bones to the pile. An old British destroyer, H.M.S. *Sabre,* built by Stephen in 1918, among the most famous of the many ships famous for their share in this week, on emerging from the harbour found some men struggling in the water. "Having no boats, for all her boats were with the first-lieutenant lifting men from the beach, she manœuvred alongside each man in turn and picked them up. While doing this she was repeatedly dive-bombed."

There seems to be little doubt that this bombing was the worst during the operation. It caused ruin on the pier and a chaos of burning and wreckage among the ships. Lieutenant Robert Bill, D.S.O., R.N., by a swift, sailor-like decision, saved the harbour entrance from being blocked by wrecks.

At 6 that evening the ship *King Orry* coming in found the harbour occupied only by burning and sinking ships; there were no soldiers on the pier and no ships moving. She stayed there till after midnight, at first under heavy bombing. Some hospital ships were very heavily bombed at 6.30. At 7 a report was passed that the harbour entrance was blocked by wreck. Luckily this rumour was false. By 7 the fury of the bombing was over; the harbour was not much bombed after dark.

The surf had made boat-work impossible at certain places on the beach, and very difficult and exhausting elsewhere. Some had been done.

The boats of H.M.S. *Jaguar* took off troops from Bray beach "for fourteen or sixteen hours continuously, the boats' crews going without food, wet through and subject to frequent bombing attacks". Four hundred men were brought off from Bray to the s.s. *Bideford*. While these were coming aboard a bomb struck the ship abaft all, and blew forty feet off her stern. Surgeon-Lieutenant John Jordan, M.B., R.N., though his sick-berth attendant was seriously wounded, stayed in the sick-bay and dealt with some fifty casualties, many of them horribly mutilated or dangerously wounded, and performed several major operations. He was helped by George William Crowther of the 6th Field Ambulance, who had been embarked from Bray beach and volunteered to help the surgeon. When the other unwounded troops had been transferred to another ship he said he would stay by the *Bideford*, "knowing her to be aground and unlikely to reach England". She did reach Eng-

land. The *Locust* gave her a thirty-hour tow; she
reached Dover on the 31st. H.M.S. *Calcutta* had her
boats in the surf all day on this day as on the day
before. H.M.S. *Vanquisher* made a record of two
round trips during the day.

All who were on the beaches learned this day that
the enemy had drawn a good deal nearer on both
sides; he had captured Mardyck Fort to the west and
occupied Nieuport to the east. Rumours came in
from enemy sources that he meant to employ "four
air divisions against us" this day, and that he meant
to attack English aerodromes and eastern seaports
that afternoon. This may have been a crude attempt
to keep our Air Force in England while he over-
whelmed us on the beach. Certainly our air observers
saw that he was bringing up his armies. Eighty tanks
and large columns of lorries were seen approaching
from the north and the east. The surrender of the
Belgian Army had released against us an enemy col-
umn three miles long which was coming down upon
us from Belgium. One sailor passing along the coast
that night picked up three soldiers from a raft. He
saw fires burning all along the Belgian coast, four
great fires burning in Dunquerque, and a line of
ships stretching twenty or thirty miles along the coast,
bringing troops away. Here and there great black
patches of oil on the water marked the graves of ships
or aeroplanes. It was reckoned that about 38,000
troops were lifted on this day. Considering the bad-
ness of the surf and the bombing, this was not a bad

total. The losses had been great. Three destroyers and four troopships had been sunk, eight other ships sunk or badly damaged, and eleven severely shaken by bombs and needing instant repair. The glass was rising; weather reports from out at sea showed that there was a chance of calm water on the morrow.

Thursday, the 30th of May.

The weather was now improving; the light wind was almost easterly and the surf gone. The engineers could now start to build piers into the sea from the beaches. They built these with army lorries and whatever deckings, scantlings and gratings could be found. These piers were of much use to the soldiers going off in boats. The boats could lie alongside them and the men no longer had to wade out waist-deep to get aboard them. The naval beach-parties, who had passed three days in the water helping men into boats, now had a slight, very slight, improvement in their lot. Some of the small paddle-steamers and other craft engaged in the lifting tried to come alongside these piers. This was not a success. The pier-ends were not sufficiently firm to stand the strain. Invention was being tried along the beaches. Grass-line was sent for; various devices were tried for heaving off strings of boats together on messengers of grass-line. Some masters tried the device of butting small ships head-on into the beach, and then drawing up to the

sterns of these ships, so that soldiers might use the
lesser ships as gangways to the bigger. These devices
sometimes worked and sometimes failed, according
to the local conditions and the skill of the men. Our
seamen, indeed, the seamen of all races, are ready, re-
sourceful men. The condition of the B.E.F., with its
left flank laid open by the Belgian surrender, called
for all the invention and resource within the race.

The wrecks from the day before had made the harbour entrance difficult; still, it could be used by one
ship at a time. Early in the morning a store-ship came
alongside the East Pier with necessary provisions.
The boxes of food blocked the pier for a time. One
well-known Channel steamer, the *Princess Maud,* on
this day noted the number of wrecks and the narrow-
ness of the swept channel by which ships came and
went; it varied from 250 to 490 feet; this did not give
much room for error in a crowded way, subject to
violent currents, in which all sorts of accidents to
steering gear might happen at any instant. One such
accident came to her. "A salvo of shells knocked a
hole in the engine-room a yard square." The men got
mattresses into the hole and "prevented a great deal
of water from entering". She had to turn back for repairs, which took some days. On her way back she
noted "wreckage, rafts and numerous craft of all
kinds" plying on the route. By this time the nation
was awake to the glory of the effort, and Dynamo was
in the triumph of its swing. Nearly eight hundred
small craft had been called to the work, with an un-

reckoned number of ships' boats. These were now plying to and fro along the dangerous and glorious narrow alley, under bombings and shell-fire from an over-armed enemy. The change in the weather raised hope in every heart. What the embarkation meant on this day can be judged from a quotation from a diary for this day.

"We proceeded to walk into the sea to embark in two boats at 10.30 p.m. After rowing for three hours, having tried to board two warships which moved away just before we could hail them, we boarded a mine-sweeper at 2 a.m. At 3 a.m. she ran aground and we transferred to another mine-sweeper."

At one time during this day 4,000 troops were embarked within the hour. As the sea was calm much greater loads could be carried in each ship. One destroyer, following the precedent set at Boulogne, took 1,400 men in one trip; it made her a bit of a handful, but all went well. The yacht *Conidaw,* which had so distinguished herself at Calais, a ship eighty feet long, over-all, made a trip with eighty soldiers in addition to her crew. Some of the best beach-work was done by some Dutch skoots and Belgian mail-packet ships with English naval crews. This was the fifth consecutive day of the adventure. The seamen reckoned it the last of the worst days. By this time some of the destroyers' crews were nearly exhausted, for they had hardly slept since the operation began. Some spare hands were distributed among them. They had not been asked for. The naval ratings had but one thought, to get to Dover with a load, and then get back to Dunquerque for another. In all, on this day, 45,955 men were lifted. Five ships were damaged, and the *King Orry,* a sixth ship, badly hit, foundered on getting out of the harbour. The cook of the *Bystander* (Mr. J. H. Elton) was on the deck of his ship at the time. As the *King Orry* sank he saw at once that many of the troops in her were much too exhausted to swim. Many of the men embarked on this day had suffered a great deal in the ten days before they embarked. Mr. Elton dived overboard with a rope to save them and remained in the water for thirty minutes, during which he rescued twenty-five officers and men. On coming aboard again he went to his galley (which was equipped with cooking utensils for seven) and in the next half-hour supplied ninety-seven soldiers with hot tea and food.

Haze and low-flying cloud made the enemy bombing much less effective on this day. Another thing which contributed a great deal to the comparatively small list of losses was the extraordinary, resolute valour of our fighting Air Force, which on this day surpassed itself by wrecking seventy-six enemy 'planes with a loss of five of its own. One patrol shot down twenty-one; one squadron of twelve shot down nineteen. One seaman noted in his diary for this day: "Things getting worse, but everybody happy."

Perhaps it was on this day (I have been unable to fix the date) that Mr. B. A. Smith, in the motor-boat *Constant Nymph,* with a crew of two, who had never before been to sea, ferried off about 800 men to two skoots. After this he collected boats that were drifting round, and towed other boatloads off amid bombing and shelling.

Friday, the 31st of May.

During the night the enemy laid a great many magnetic mines by air along all the approaches to the harbour. These were added anxieties, but not very fatal. He had brought up more batteries and was now shelling the beaches more heavily from both sides. All through the night the transports sailed. When morning dawned the beaches were nearly clear, though more troops were on the road and pressing into the area. The troops of the First French Army were due to begin to embark this morning.

Just after sunrise the easterly wind freshened. At once the surf began to run upon the beaches and boats capsized. Early in the day the jetty at Bray, newly-built of lorries, was broken by the surf and shell-fire combined. The enemy had by this time come further west along the beaches. He had now guns in battery, with which he could shell all the Zuydecoote Pass. A good many light craft were sunk. By this time the boat service on the beaches had much improved. There were more whalers, and a very large number of small power-boats, which did much better than the miscellaneous ship's boats in use hitherto.

One ship was sunk during this day and two damaged.

While the surf was running Captain W. A. Young, commanding the *Levenwood,* of 800 tons, was asked to put the nose of his ship into the sand and to keep steaming slowly ahead so as to avoid going broadside on in the rising tide. In this position he got out a "messenger" or revolving hawser to the shore, and sent boats in and out by it. He was bombed all the time while in this position, but none of the bombs fell nearer to him than 100 yards. Mr. Moodey, one of his firemen, kept going over the side and swimming to the wading soldiers. He encouraged those who could swim to strike out to the boats. He swam back with the too weary men who might have collapsed; he actually carried or supported all those who could not swim. He did this for three hours in a heavy swell and surf.

One very great benefit received during this day was a ship-load of collapsible boats and pontoons.

This day's surf, having displaced, soon broke up the derelict lorries which had been used in the building of the pier. The broken relics washed about in the breakers and were a great danger to the boats. Other sources of very great danger were drifting clothing and grassline. Thousands of soldiers' greatcoats were floating. These fouled the screws of the motor-boats, which were then frequently made unmanageable and swamped in the surf. The surf was "Less dangerous during the afternoon," as two seamen note.

During the afternoon, H.M.S. *Skipjack,* when filled with troops and towing a motor-boat, was attacked by dive-bombers. She shot down three aircraft, but five bombs from one plane struck her. She turned over and sank. The survivors were picked up by a neighbouring destroyer and reached Dover. One man writing of this day says: "Ammunition was going up like fireworks. I waded out to my armpits and scrambled aboard a boat. Two others jumped out of the boat and completely swamped her. We spent about two hours trying to re-float her, but the seas were too strong. I decided to look for a change of clothes and searched the beach, where I soon picked up some short pants and socks. On returning, I found my party gone. I picked up some biscuits on the beach and presently, when I boarded the destroyer, I had an enormous feast of bread, bully-beef and tea."

Another man writes: "We reached the East Jetty at 11 p.m. On one place there had been a direct hit on the Mole. The gap had been patched with boards. A final halt was made 200 yards from the end, which was altogether about a mile long. Most of the men laid down on the jetty and went to sleep in spite of the cold. A German bomber flew over us at one o'clock, dropping bombs. The battalion just behind us was heavily shelled and machine-gunned and suffered severe casualties. Two ships had already been sunk at the end of the jetty. It was apparently impossible to embark till the tide rose.

"At five o'clock a destroyer drew alongside. It was

daylight, but luckily there was a mist. We were conducted below and all were very soon asleep."

All through the day there were the usual heavy bombings by the enemy. They were frequently sending over companies of bombers twenty-five or thirty strong, supported by fighters. During all this day our great effort in the air was against the German forces advancing from the east and west. In the evening our bombers dropped over sixty tons of bombs on Germans approaching from the east. One squadron dropped eight tons of bombs on Germans advancing towards Furnes and another company dropped ten tons of bombs an assemblies of tanks moving towards Cassel. Unfortunately, the troops inside the Dunquerque lines could not have the comfort of watching these attacks.

One shipmaster, writing of this day, says: "We soon had about 200 soldiers on board. The stewards were employed getting food for men who had had but one meal in the last three days. The doctor, who was Jewish, on being told that there was pork in the stew, said, 'I do not care if there are dead dogs in it, I'm going to have my share'. The homeward route was a wonderful sight. Hundreds of small craft of every description, making towards Dunquerque. The German bombers were busy dropping their loads all over the place. There were more than seventy enemy planes overhead dropping their bombs all round on us, like hail-stones, but our luck held good. We escaped undamaged. The gunner put in some great

work with his gun and hit three enemy planes, two
of which came down. I was just coming along Folke-
stone pier at 8.30, when a violent explosion occurred.
Another lucky escape. A mine had gone off behind
us. We had brought home 504 troops, seventy of
them French."

It was a most successful day for those lifting troops.
59,797 were brought to England.

Among the remarkable feats of the day must be
mentioned that of Able-Seaman S. Palmer, in the
thirty-foot motor-yacht *Maid Errant*. Putting into the
beach in the surf, she was rushed and swamped by
French soldiers. She was then washed ashore. He re-
floated her. He had no crew, save one stoker, but he
gathered a British N.C.O. and eight soldiers and with
these put off for England. The engine was not working well and at last broke down. He then broke up
the wood fittings of the yacht, into paddles, and in-
duced the eight soldiers to paddle. He reached Dover
safely and set forth again the next day for another
trip, but was stopped, as it was felt that the *Maid
Errant* was too slow for the work.

Saturday, the 1st of June.

On this day the enemy made his most determined
effort to ruin the lifting. The Master Mariner had
written on the 30th that things were getting worse;
they now became much worse. From midnight until

five in the morning, the shelling increased to such a pitch that of the two hospital ships sent in for wounded, only one was able to go in to bring them off. The other lay off the harbour entrance for four hours, but could not get in. Four troopships tried to get in, and failed. One entered at dawn, loaded up, and was returning, when she was heavily bombed. Our troops were out of La Panne, but enemy shells fell there.

At five o'clock the enemy let lose a monstrous air attack all over the area. It lasted for four hours, with successions of aeroplanes thirty to forty strong; one Master Mariner made the note, "Over 100 bombs on ships near here since 5.30". We were making, or hoping to make a very great effort, to lift the rest of the armies on this day; the enemy was bent on stopping us. We tried all the routes. All were now under very heavy shell-fire. It was reckoned that the enemy had at least three batteries of six-inch guns near Gravelines, besides the heavy coastal guns in Fort Grand Philippe. The French ships, using this approach, were much shelled; several were sunk. At six that evening the signal was sent from the harbour, "Things are getting very hot for ships". It was decided that the harbour could no longer be used during daylight. A naval officer had the heart-breaking task of telling the men waiting on the jetty that they would have to go back and wait for night to fall. During the darkness a great effort was to be made; small ships were to take men from the beaches to the east; about a hundred small French ships were to take French soldiers from the beach at Malo; we were to have twenty-four ships, as well as power-boats, at and inside the jetty; the French were to send ships to the Quai of the new outer harbour. This meant, that between 9 p.m. and 3 a.m. something like two hundred and fifty small vessels would be at sea in a narrow channel without beacons or navigating lights, with all the officers overstrained, all the ships over-loaded, all the crews overworked, on a night of last quarter-moon, as black as a summer night can be, in waters with considerable current, certain to be sown with mines, all of them under shell-fire, and likely to be bombed. The burning buildings in the ruins of Dunquerque were the only lights that guided those mariners. The Admiral from Dover controlled the traffic; a Dutch naval officer and Dutch crew, under Commander Maund, led the ships in.

The lifting on this day was a record; we took away 61,998 men in spite of the appalling fire. Our loss in troopships, destroyers and mine-sweepers sunk and damaged was very heavy.

By this time many soldiers had learned something of the management of boats in sea-ways; they were of much help during this day. All day long upon the beaches the boats were plying under continual dive-bombing and machine-gunning. Many boats were sunk or capsized by these attacks. In those parts of the beach where there was surf (and there was always surf somewhere) a capsizing caused confusion, from men being unable to swim, or so wounded that they could not swim. The dive-bombers flew over the water machine-gunning all that they saw. Men on the beaches replied with Bren guns.

One ship leaving the pier with a thousand men on board was attacked by eighteen dive-bombers. The bombs killed forty and wounded two hundred and forty of those on deck. She had three doctors on board, "but it was very difficult to treat the wounded owing to the crowd. An oil-pipe was burst in the engine-room; the ship had to be towed, but presently could proceed under her own steam". Our Air Force again did heroic deeds all day. One squadron at about noon on this day attacked a formation of between fifty and sixty enemy fighters and drove them all in-land; another squadron engaged a formation of eighty.

Among the countless gallant deeds of those days the work of the two fine motor-boats *Marasole* and *Pauleteer* must be mentioned. These were in charge of Mr. D. T. Banks, who began in the *Marasole* with a crew of two ordinary seamen, a Bren gun, a Lewis gun, "and a compass which he did not know how to use". He completed seven or eight trips, and brought back more than four hundred men. When the *Marasole* was sunk he continued with the *Pauleteer* under frequent machine-gun fire. At times he took a run ashore in Dunquerque, then burning fiercely and under intense bombing.

More than one observer mentions the scene upon the crowded routes. "All sorts of craft were coming round the buoy, all fully loaded with troops. A batch of about twenty Belgian fishing-boats bore down, the leader asking us the way to England. I sung out the course, and told him to follow the other traffic and he would be all right."

The log of H.M.S. *Sandown*, Commander K. M. Greig, D.S.O., R.N., for this day may be quoted:

02.35. Anchored off the N. Goodwin Sands in response S.O.S. from *Golden Gift* ashore high and dry with 250 troops on board.
Took off troops in motor-boat in five trips and returned to Ramsgate to disembark troops.

11.00. Proceeded to Bray and anchored there 14.30. Shelling from Nieuport batteries. Embarked 900 British troops. Heavy air attacks and 6-in. shelling throughout afternoon, necessitating shifting billet on two occasions.

23.30. Weighed. Two magnetic mines dropped by plane close to.

5.00. Disembarked troops.

Remarks. Embarking troops was carried out under difficult circumstances owing to heavy shelling, air attacks and swell running, which made boat-work very arduous. The spirit of the officers and men was excellent. Ratings volunteered from the stokehold for any duties required.

On this day seventy-eight enemy aeroplanes were destroyed over the Dunquerque beaches.

Sunday, the 2nd of June.

Very early in the morning some of the men from Bergues marched to the end of the Mole, which they reached just before daylight. There they found a fully-laden ship casting off for home. The naval officers told the men that they had better go back to the beaches before daylight, to be safe from air attack. "The return to the beach was very slow; the Mole was long, all ranks were exhausted and hungry, and there were two lines of troops, the French on the left, the British on the right, and when our men moved back to the beaches, the French were still moving forward towards the sea." (They were being lifted by the French.) The disappointed men marched back to the beach, and there some of them launched a boat from a derelict oil-tanker and got aboard a French drifter, which anchored in the Road, and endured many bombing attacks, till she was fully loaded. The rest of the battalion dug themselves into a canal bank, till night, when they came away in a destroyer.

Another unit, which had fired its last rounds, destroyed its guns and wrecked its wireless sets, was also turned back from the Mole end, and passed a dreary day of bombing and shelling at Malo. "Malo was packed with thousands of deserted vehicles. The Mole (the East Pier) is about 1¾ miles long, and stands twenty feet above the water. Accurate salvoes of 5.9's continued every ten minutes, but they only shelled one end at a time. There were always plenty of gaps in the Mole." These troops got away a little later than those mentioned above.

This day being Sunday, a Chaplain held Holy Communion on the beach and dunes. His congregation was scattered five times by low-diving bombers, but reassembled each time till the service ended.

As an anticyclone was now centred over England, the Channel was calm, with a good deal of haze. What light breaths blew tended to carry the smoke of the burning city over the harbour entrance and its approaches; it was very difficult for mariners to see their way in.

There had been much fighting in the perimeter during the last few days; at Furnes and at Bergues many men had been wounded. It was felt that possibly some of these grievously hurt men might be permitted to leave without molestation. The Geneva Convention, which provides for the safe passage of hospital ships carrying none but wounded soldiers, had been accepted by Germany. An appeal was therefore clearly wirelessed at 10.30 this morning. "Wounded situation acute and Hospital Ships to enter during day. Geneva Convention will be honourably observed and it is felt that the enemy will refrain from attacking."

Hospital carriers had already suffered a good deal during the lifting, though showing the illuminated Red Cross and flying Red Cross flags. Their logs say "The vessel was heavily bombed; eight hands reported suffering from shell-shock. The attacks on these hospital ships were deliberate."

"On one occasion, at 8.15 on the 31st, she had seven separate air attacks. A magnetic mine fell so close that we had to reverse to avoid. Twenty minutes later another mine blew up less than a hundred yards ahead. It partially lifted the ship out of the water. Another dropped ahead only four feet away, but did not explode. We were continually worried by aircraft."

After the wireless message had been issued, two hospital ships, the *Paris* and the *Worthing*, sailed to bring off the wounded. The *Worthing* was attacked by twelve bombers and forced to return. At 7.15 p.m. the *Paris* reported that she was bombed, badly hit and in danger. Tugs were sent to her, but she was sinking, and went down after midnight. The bombing which wrecked her took place in full daylight, somewhere about 7 p.m. Men in a ship just astern of her at the time "saw the German aeroplanes machine-gunning the boats which contained nurses and medical personnel." A Master Mariner who went to the rescue says: "We had a job of work with the hospital ships. *Paris* survivors had been bombed and machine-gunned. Rendered assistance to ninety-five survivors, including five nurses who were seriously wounded." He adds that: "Most of the ships which went into Dunquerque were hit more or less badly. In most of them their compasses were disorganized by explosions, and they were difficult to steer and often leaky."

As these last atrocities made it impossible for us to take certain of the more grievously wounded men, it was decided that chaplains, doctors and orderlies should draw lots, as on past occasions, for the honour of staying to look after them. The lots were drawn; the wounded were left in charge of those to whom the lots fell. So far as I can learn they have not yet been exchanged.

An observer writes: "The sky was absolutely black from burning oil; the air was full of black, oily smuts; all the sea was edged and coated with smut; the men were either black with oil-smut or splashed with grey mud flung up by shells between the tide-marks. What struck me most was the number of French and Belgian dogs which had attached themselves to the armies. It was sad to see them trying to come on board the ships. Hundreds of them were shot." A good many were brought to England, and their quarantine money subscribed for by the troops.

At about 4.45 that afternoon, three of the R.A.F. fighters sighted three enemy formations near Dunquerque. Each of these formations was about a dozen bombers, cruising around in great circles from which, from time to time, single bombers swooped down to bomb and shoot at the trawlers and boats.

The three R.A.F. fighters split up, to attack.

One went straight at a bomber just climbing from an attack and shot it down into the sea. He then went at a second bomber and shot that down, too. He then went at a third and put it down out of control. On rising from this third flight, the airman found the enemy all gone, except for one bomber making for the shelter of clouds.

The second of the three R.A.F. men attacked and chased two of the enemy bombers over Dunquerque. One of them plunged out of control into the smoke of the burning city. The airman then turned to attack about twenty bombers still circling over the approaches; he at once attacked them and put one down, damaged.

The third R.A.F. man meanwhile attacked a group of three enemy bombers. His battle was taken over by three other British fighters; he rejoined his two original companions, and with them drove off two bombers which attacked them.

Soon afterwards, the three saw below them two big ship's boats, full of troops, not under way. Two of our fighters went to find help for these boats, while the third cruised above them, to guard them. Eight enemy planes attacked him; he went for all the eight, and drove the formation back over Dunquerque.

These three fighters had shot down two enemies

certainly; they judged that two others never flew again, and three others were damaged, one, very severely. Not one of the three fighters had been hit. The two fighters found help for the boats. Two tugs came up to look after them, and brought them into safety. Fifty-six enemy aeroplanes were shot down over the beaches on this day.

Soon after this, the great lifting of the day began. We sent in sixty vessels with many boats. The French sent in ten ships and 120 fishing boats. A great effort was needed, for the line was now very short; the enemy was pressing on the French garrison towards Uxem, and sending guns along the beach to shell the pier.

While going back with a load of troops that evening, the *Royal Daffodil* was attacked by six enemy aircraft. Five salvoes missed her; a bomb from the sixth went through three of her decks into the engine-room, and then out through the starboard side before bursting; the engines stopped; the enemy 'planes machine-gunned the ship and set her on fire. She was by this time listing heavily to starboard. Her Master, Captain G. Johnson, very promptly shifted all her gear to port, lowered all her port boats into the sea and let them fill with water. The weight thus brought to port tilted the hole clear of the sea. While some put out the fire, her two engineers, Mr. J. Coulthard and Mr. W. Evans, took all the beds they could find and plugged the hole with them. When the leak was thus checked, Mr. Evans stood up to the neck in

water, holding open a bilge-valve, while Mr. Coulthard kept the pumps going. In this way they reached
Ramsgate, "the engines going very slowly, as the
Diesel had three parts of water to one of oil." She
landed her seamen safely, probably about 1,500 in
this trip. In all this ship brought away 8,000 men.

On board her at the time was "the soldier W. C. E.
Smith, R.A.M.C., who did excellent work, attending
to the sick and wounded." He won from the captain
such a tribute as few men can ever hope to win. "I
have never seen a soldier at sea play the part of a
sailor so well. He behaved in a most gallant manner
the whole time. . . . When there is no doctor on board
it makes it doubly difficult."

One of the wounded tells me that he lay on a
stretcher on the sand for two days close to Dunquerque, "in a cloud of grey smoke," and heard the
shells going over all day and all night long. He was
taken off by a destroyer on this night.

During all this last period, our men were holding
the line outside the eastern side of Dunquerque,
helped by fire from destroyers in the Road. We were
taking very great numbers of French troops, for
nearly all our men had gone. The last men in the line
were called out of it that night; at 11.30 p.m. the
Senior Naval Officer reported "B.E.F. evacuated."

In all, 31,427 men had been brought away that
day, with a loss of one hospital ship and two trawlers
sunk; and one hospital ship, one cruiser, one destroyer and one trawler severely damaged. Of course,

few ships escaped without receiving damage of some kind.

At eight on this evening one of our transports sighted a sailing barge in need of help. Several sailing barges had been used in the service, having good capacity and small draught. This one now contained only soldiers, who had somehow sailed her over almost to the Goodwins without any sailors. What had become of her crew? Possibly, she had been towed to Dunquerque without a crew; she was now towed home to safety.

In the account of this day something must be written of the loss of Commander Clouston, R.N., who had for six anxious days been "doing noble service on the jetty at Dunquerque."

On Saturday night he returned to Dover to report upon the situation and to receive final orders for the great lifting of troops planned for Sunday night. He left Dover on this day in a motor-launch with a naval officer and some seamen. A second motor-launch came with them. On their way they were attacked by enemy aircraft, who put his motor-launch out of action and left her in a sinking condition. Commander Clouston waved to the men in the second launch to get away before they were sunk. With the naval officer, the only survivor of his Company, he then left his wrecked launch to try to swim to a boat seen a couple of miles away. Becoming weary long before he could reach this boat he turned to swim back to the water-logged launch, and was never seen again. His companion, after swimming for two or three hours, reached the boat he had sighted and with great difficulty got on board her. She proved to be a ship's deserted cutter. In this he drifted for some time till picked up by a French trawler which had lost her way in the Channel. He undertook to navigate this trawler back to Ramsgate, and did so. Later he reported at Dover dressed in clothes borrowed from a French sailor.

Commander Clouston had been of the utmost service in helping the escape of nearly two hundred thousand men under frightful conditions of strain and danger. It was a grief to many that he did not live to see the lifting brought to an end.

Monday, the 3rd of June.

Early in this day, the R.A.F. sent large patrols over the Dunquerque area. They found no enemy targets, aircraft or troop columns, in the district. They went on to Bergues and Gravelines to bomb the batteries which had been so very grievous to us. The bombing was heavy; no gun fired from Bergues for a considerable time afterwards.

We urged the French to make every effort to end the lifting during this night. The anticyclone, which had given a blessed calm during the critical days of the lifting, was now slowly edging to the north. The wind was north-easterly, making an unpleasant and dangerous jobble at the harbour entrance. The fine weather haze thickened into fog, so that several ships had to anchor in the Road.

The fog and smoke were a hindrance to us and to the enemy. His airmen and gunners made great efforts to see what was going on by firing star-shells and flares over the dangerous approach just east of the harbour entrance, where the traffic and the wrecks were thickest. Besides the old known wrecks on the charts, there were now at least twelve others, three to the west, nine to the east, seven of them in the fairway; more wrecks lay in the harbour. Ships had to hang about at the entrance in the jobble of the tide, trying to keep clear of wrecks and traffic till they were signalled to enter. Even inside the entrance, in the darkness, ships were frequently banging into each other or into the jetty as one left and another took a berth.

H.M.S. *Express* and H.M.S. *Shikari* were the last ships to leave, H.M.S. *Express* at 3.18, H.M.S. *Shikari* at 3.40. The enemy tried to bomb H.M.S. *Shikari;* luckily, the haze made the aim poor. These two ships carried between them about one thousand soldiers and the British pier parties. The only troops now remaining in Dunquerque were some non-combatants of the garrison, and the few units still holding the fortress for the French. After the last ships had left, some motor-boats, containing the last of the British naval ratings, went through the harbour to make sure that all had been brought away. For some days past, demo-

lition parties had been blowing up harbour equipment which might serve the enemy; this work was
now done, as far as possible. Some of the enemy had
now crept right into Dunquerque; some of them fired
from time to time, with their automatics. The naval
officers were struck by the silence which had fallen
after the racket and roar of the last week; now there
came only a shot or two now and then. As the last
boat left the port an officer in her was shocked by the
mess and disorder. This had been a great and busy
seaport, full of order and industry; now it was a filthy,
black, smouldering heap of ruins, with dead ships in
the harbour and at both sides of the entrance, dead
men floating in the sea, and washing up to the beach;
the wrecks of aeroplanes lying about, and an incon-
ceivable litter of broken transport, packing-cases, old
clothes and smashed weapons. He had a horror of
leaving all this mess not cleared up and made tidy.
He had been in charge of the beach since the operation began. Neither he nor any of the naval ratings
under him had had any rest to speak of for eight or
nine days. As he went out he thought of the thing
which had so impressed him on one of his visits at
dawn, of the great black formations of men patiently
waiting on the sands. Through his work and that of
our seamen all those patient men had been taken
away.

An Admiralty message ended the Operation Dynamo at 2.23 P.M.

Though the lifting was finished, some useful cruising was done later, to pick up stragglers. The R.A.F. and a number of motor-boats cruised over the Channel, and helped to find and save men wrecked in a transport and in a barge.

Some French soldiers were lifted from Dunquerque harbour during the next midnight, by French and English ships, the last ship (the *Princess Maud*) leaving at 1.50 on the 4th. As she left, a shell fell in the berth she had occupied a moment before.

It is said that the white flag was hoisted on the ruins of Dunquerque at nine o'clock that morning.

On the 5th, a motor-boat picked up thirty-three French soldiers and two naval ratings. A few more drifting soldiers were picked up by patrols during the next few days. About 1,100 came to England in small parties in Belgian and French trawlers. Many strange escapes were made. A French lieutenant arrived at Dunquerque with nineteen men; they embarked in a boat and got aboard a wrecked passenger-ship lying in two fathoms of water. Here they camped without food or drink for a week, making fires of wood. Four of them built a raft, went off in her, and were seen no more. Seven others died of thirst and exposure. In the evening of June the 12th, the survivors were seen by a British aeroplane, who reported them to the patrols; a motor-boat went out at once and brought off the lieutenant and eight men, with their rifles and kit. These must have been among the last to be saved.

The numbers lifted and brought to England from Dunquerque alone during the operation were:

British	186,587
French	123,095
Brought by hospital ships, etc.	6,981
	316,663

THE lifting was a wonderful improvisation by the seamen of this people. The landsmen played their parts, too, from the Staff Officer, who spent twelve hours of one day up to the waist in water, helping to push off boats, to the oarsmen, who volunteered to bear a hand.

The Masters of ninety-one merchant ships, of fifty-seven passenger- and store-ships, and of thirty-four tugs were thanked for their share in the work. One authority says that 665 small craft were employed off the beaches, as well as a great number of ships' boats. The Port of London alone sent thirty-four motor life-boats and 881 ships' boats. "These small craft lifted more than 100,000 men." "No boat ceased work as long as troops were in sight on shore." "As the boats were sunk, the crews went elsewhere, into other boats, and carried on." Of the civilians working there, four were killed and two wounded. Of the merchant seamen engaged, 125 were killed and eighty-one wounded. Six English and seven French destroyers were sunk. 171 English ships were repaired during the operation. Many of the repairs were of a serious kind, as in the case of the *Royal Daffodil,* yet the work was done so quickly that the ship returned to the task. "About 1,000 charts were issued; 600 of these had routes laid off on them for those who had no equipment."

"Many of the boats had not even a compass and no navigational instruments other than a lead pencil, and if they once lost contact with their convoy their chance of getting there in the strong currents was very slight. . . . Some boats got to Calais, instead of Dunquerque, where they received a rousing reception from the Boche."

"Many of the boats were from the Thames Estuary. They had never before left the Estuary, and only one of their crews had been further than Ramsgate, but the conduct of the crews of all these boats was exemplary. One 35-foot motor-launch ferried off 600 men to transports and carried 420 direct to England."

Such an assemblage of destroyers, drifters, danlayers, Dutch trawlers and skoots, mine-sweepers, ferry-boats, tugs, river and pleasure steamers has never before plied the Channel. The London tug *Nicholas Drew* went there towing twelve life-boats; the famous London fire-boat, the *Massey Shaw,* went with a fire service crew, brought off sixty men and carried them to England. Later, with a naval crew, she tenderedoff some hundreds, then carried home forty-six and returned to the beach for more. At the home ports 670 troop trains carried the soldiers away. Volunteer war workers provided mobile canteens to all these trains, to give food, drink, sweets and cigarettes to all, and to send off telegrams for those who wished.

What the service could be may be judged by the following. On the 1st of June, one ship, crossing to Dunquerque, was six times attacked by dive-bombers. While alongside at the jetty, she was attacked again. On leaving, full of men, she was attacked twelve times, and so much damaged that she had to anchor for ninety minutes while she repaired her steam-pipes. During these ninety minutes she was attacked continuously. She then returned home. Yet under these conditions many ships made several trips. The old destroyer, H.M.S. *Sabre,* made nine trips; H.M.S. *Malcolm* made eight trips; the *Royal Daffodil* made seven, and was turned back from an eighth; H.M.S. *Codrington* made seven trips. The *Leda* and the *Medway Queen* seven each; H.M.S. *Shikari* and H.M.S. *Vanquisher,* seven each; H.M.S. *Vanquisher* and many others making two on one day. Many ships made six trips. H.M.S. *Princess Elizabeth* worked without stopping for four days and nights. I have mentioned the endurance of the thirty naval officers and 320 naval ratings employed ashore as beach-parties; how living a strength is generosity! Most of the destroyers' crews worked to the very brink of exhaustion; in some ships of the Channel ferry services the crews went on till they dropped.

Hundreds of little vessels from half the coast of England deserve to have their names in the Navy henceforward.

The enemy had proclaimed our complete encircle-
ment and destruction; no doubt he had expected to
achieve both aims. He did not do these things, because he could not. He came up against inundations
and defences which checked his tanks: against soldiers who defied him and drove him back: against
our Air Force, which attacked him with complete in-
difference to the numbers he sent against it: and
against our Navy, which is a service apart. Lastly, he
came up against the spirit of this Nation, which,
when roused, will do great things. The Nation rose
to the lifting of the Armies as to no other event in
recent times. It was an inspiration to all, to feel that
will to save running through the land. The event was
as swift as Life; no possible preparation could be
made; the thing fell suddenly, and had to be met on
the instant. Instantly, in reply to the threat, came the
will to help from the whole marine population of
these islands. Word passed that the armies were ship-
wrecked on the sands; at once the lifeboats put out,
and kept plying as long as there was anyone to lift.

Our Army did not save Belgium; that is a little
matter compared with the great matter, that it tried
to. In the effort, it lost thirty thousand men, all its
transport, all its guns, all its illusions; it never lost its
heart.

The Nation said to those men, in effect: "Hold on;
we will get you away." They held on, and we got
them away.

It is hard to think of those dark formations on the

sand, waiting in the rain of death, without the knowledge, that Hope and Help are stronger things than death. Hope and Help came together in their power into the minds of thousands of simple men, who went out in the Operation Dynamo and plucked them from ruin.

I thank those officers of the Army who have permitted me to quote half a dozen vivid paragraphs from their diaries.

I am deeply indebted to Air Commodore Peake, of the Air Ministry, for the welcome and help given to my plans by him. I thank Mr. J. C. Nerney, the Librarian of the Air Ministry, for looking out for me so much that had to be studied.

I thank Captain Brooking, R.N., for a delightful and busy afternoon at the Admiralty, making a first acquaintance with the Operation Dynamo.

It is difficult for me to express my thanks to Vice-Admiral Sir Bertram Ramsay, K.C.B., M.V.O., for his never-failing help, when already sufficiently occupied by bombardment from the enemy and the possibilities of invasion. I am grateful for all the information he has given me and for the track-chart supplied by him to make the jacket for this book.

I am deeply indebted to Captain F. W. Bush, D.S.O., D.S.C., R.N., for his most moving account of things seen at Dunquerque. I thank Commander K. M. Greig, D.S.O., R.N., Lieutenant R. Bill, D.S.O.,

R.N., Lieutenant-Commander R. C. Wardrop, R.N., Lieutenant-Commander P. F. Cammiade, R.N., and Sub-Lieutenant J. Mason, R.N., for clearing up doubtful points and helping me to understand what happened off the French coast in that critical time.

I thank Lieutenant H. Powell, R.N.V.R., for his clear photograph of the Dynamo Room, where this great Operation was planned and kept going.

I thank Miss Marjorie Bell for her help with the official photographs used as illustrations.

I warmly thank Mr. B. E. Bellamy and Mr. W. G. Hynard, of the Ministry of Shipping, for making my work there so easy and so pleasant.

I thank Mr. N. K. Johnson, D.Sc., the Director of the Meteorological Office, for letting me consult the weather charts for the vital days of the campaign. Perhaps the weather which gave the enemy so much advantage did at last help to save us from ruin.

I thank Mrs. Roxbee, Miss Taylor and Miss Walton, for patient copying, and for the accuracy, neatness and quickness of all their work.

I must not end this list without thanking some who have been particularly helpful in other ways; among these let me name Mrs. Hamilton and Mr. A. D. Divine, both until lately of the Ministry of Information.

JOHN MASEFIELD.

To the Seamen

You seamen, I have eaten your hard bread
And drunken from your tin, and known your ways;
I understand the qualities I praise
Though lacking all, with only words instead,

I tell you this, that in the future time
When landsmen mention sailors, such, or such,
Someone will say "Those fellows were sublime
Who brought the Armies from the Germans' clutch."

Through the long time the story will be told;
Long centuries of praise on English lips,
Of courage godlike and of hearts of gold
Off Dunquerque beaches in the little ships.

And ships will dip their colours in salute
To you, henceforth, when passing Zuydecoote.

A Young English Air-Man

O smiling, sun-burned youth who rode the sky
Like to the sparrow-hawk or summer swift,
And watched your shadow flitting on the drift
Far underneath you as you hurried by,

Six months ago to-day you put off bird
To gleam as ion in a nation's will,
To save the ruined friends and then lie still,
Spring never to be touched by summer's word.

Often unseen by those you helped to save
You rode the air above that foreign dune
And died like the unutterably brave
That so your friends might see the English June.

Haply, in some sharp instant in mid-sky,
When you, at the bird's summit, took the lunge
Of the foe's bitterness that made you die,
And the bright bird declined into her plunge,

You, from the Heaven, saw, in English chalk
White, about Dover, some familiar track,
That feet of yours would never again walk
Since you were killed and never coming back,

Yet knew that your young life, as price paid over,
Let thousands live to tread that track to Dover.

Thoughts for Later On

When someone somewhere bids the bombing cease,
And ships unharassed ply at Life's demands,
And friends again greet friends in foreign lands,
And sad survivors call the ruin peace,

Then, peace will be but ruin, unless Thought
Of how the peace was purchased be in mind,
Of how, to buy it, men are lying blind
Under the sea in ruined wreckage caught;

Thinking of them, and those who rode the air,
Or shogged the Flanders plain in Belgium's aid,
Or stood at Cassel with the grand Brigade,
Peace may be filled with beauty everywhere,

If, with each purchased breath, we vow to give
To Earth the joy they never lived to live.

Not any drums nor bugles with Last Post
For these men dead in intellect's despite.
Think not of war as pageant but as blight
Famine and blasting to the pilgrim ghost.

So, for the brave men fallen for man's crime,
The young men beautiful all unfulfilled,
The broken and the mangled and the killed
For whom no Spring can come in cuckoo-time

Let there be beauty spilt like holy seed
Not any mock of custom or parade
But hope atoning for the ruin made
And shame alike for deed and want of deed.

When We Return Thanks

Ah, when the spirit knows the dewy dawn, the peace-
time,
Friend will meet fellow coming in their thousands
to the stage,
There will be quiet there in expectation of the
dancing
And a stillness as of sacring while the music plays
In unheard sweet, in unknown ways.
Ah, then, the march of destiny, that broke them, itself
breaking,
Will usher in a movement cool as of the April wheat,
And the silence of the crowd will be as spirit's dedi-
cation
And its whiteness and its tension fitting prelude to
the beat
The hushèd stress of dancer's feet.
Then, to a music like forgiveness of all evil
The dancers of the proffered chance will glide into
the light,
The immortal thought of spirits will be ours for a
moment
And the winter of our sorrow be an April of delight
If we will and do aright
With our memory brief as leaves and little hope and
feeble sight.

WAITING ON THE DUNES

ON A BEACH NEAR DUNQUERQUE   [*Photos The Times*

A SHIP-LOAD

[The Times Photo

SMOKE RISING FROM BURNING DUNQUERQUE [Keystone Press Agency

TRANSPORTS IN THE OPERATION DYNAMO [*Associated Press Photo*]

DUNQUERQUE BURNING [*Associated Press*]

DUNQUERQUE PIER [*Associated Press*

DUNQUERQUE. THE PIER ON THE LEFT [*London News Agency*